COMING OUT OF THE VALLEY

By

MKAMBANIZITHE DAKA

FOREWARD BY

BISHOP HENRY MUMBA

COMING OUT OF THE VALLEY

By MkambanizitheDaka

Copyright 2018 MkambanizitheDaka

Scriptural quotes are from New King James Version (NKJV)

ISBN: 9781718022560

For More information contact:

Email: zithebest1.27@gmail.com.

TABLE OF CONTENTS

ACKNOWLEDGEMENTS

Special gratitude to my wife Diana, thank you for supporting me and being a great encouragement in my ministry. It has been a great journey walking with you.

Bishop Henry Mumba; am grateful that you believed in me and created platforms for me to exercise my God given gifts, I get inspired just to know that I have a father that believes in me. Thank you so much for writing the foreword and all the words of encouragement

Bishop Boniface Shonga, thank you for believing and encouraging me to pursue what God has put in my life. On the 23rd of October, 2009, when I was in pain and feeling confused, you told me that my fulfillment in life was in ministry, this book is as a result of those encouraging words.

Pastor Yamish, I appreciate that you designed the cover for this book. May God refresh and grant you, your heart's desire.

I also want to express my gratitude to Sister Jacqueline Chibwe Mooba and Mrs. Mwaipopo for editing the book, my God will bless you and your families.

To all members of the Apostolic Church in Zambia, Deliverance Centre, thank you for your great supports and prayers; I am privileged to be your pastor.

My heartfelt appreciation also go to all the people that have believed and given me the opportunity to develop my God given abilities of helping people come into their great destiny. I may not mention you by name but the Lord bless you all.

Finally, special thanks to my heavenly Father who has promised to neither leave me nor forsake me, you have been faithful to me, my life is a demonstration of your love and care to all who call on your Name, I will always love and serve you because you are Dependable, there is none like you

FOREWORD

This book gives hope and shows hope to anyone going through a tough and rough time in life. It offers redemption due to wrong choices once made in life if certain things are done right. It encourages to rise above adversity in such times knowing with full conviction of God's help.

It describes how to come out of weeping and tears knowing that such a condition is temporal, if only the attitude is corrected and right things are done. Any valley we go through, works for our good when we take the right steps. I encourage every reader to soak himself or herself with the content of this book. It refreshes your spirit and energizes you with hope to go to next step in your life.

Bishop Henry Mumba

Former National Overseer for the Apostolic Church in Zambia.

INTRODUCTION

*The hand of the Lord came upon me and brought me out in the Spirit of the Lord, **and set me down in the midst of the valley;** and it was full of bones. Ezekiel 37:1 NKJV*

Valleys speak of seasons where everything seems to be going contrary to expectation; valleys also speak of periods of pain. Sometimes you hear people say "I am going through the valley, things are tough."

A valley speaks of a number of things, in this book; a valley is used to represent seasons when someone is experiencing low moments, seasons of bitterness. Valleys speak of seasons where everything seems to be going contrary to expectation; valleys also speak of periods of pain. Sometimes you hear people say "I am going through the valley, things are tough." These are times when it seems as though everyone is against you and nothing seems to make sense.

I remember a time when I had applied to get into Bible school and no response was coming from the school for more than a year, I experienced extremely painful times, friends and relatives did not understand my decision. In one of the Sunday services at a Church I attended in 1999, a preacher who had advised me to take a course in Accounts and not missions spoke during the service saying "there are some young men in this Church who are very stubborn, When we tell them to go to school, their response is 'God has called me.'" Seated in the front roll and almost everyone knew that he was talking about me, I was hurt, frustrated and I felt like quitting Church. That was my VALLEY that particular time. There are so many ways one can experience valleys in their lives; could be in marriage, politics, ministry etc. The Bible records a number of valleys that speak something about our lives. In this book, I will present the five major valleys in the Old Testament and what they mean to us, I will also show you how to come out of each type of valley.

CHAPTER ONE

THE VALLEY OF SIDDIM

And the king of Sodom, the king of Gomorrah, the king of Admah, the king of Zeboiim, and the king of Bela (that is, Zoar) ***went out and joined together in battle in the Valley of Siddim*** *against Chedorlaomer king of Elam… .Gen 14:8-9 NKJV*

In the valley of Siddim, you experience pain because of wrong choices in life.

The first valley is what is called the valley of Siddim. The valley of Siddim according to Genesis 14: 8 is the valley where the cities of Sodom and Gomorrah were located. It was full of bitumen pits and a very intense battle took place in this valley.

In this valley, you experience pain because of wrong choices in life. It is in the valley of Siddim that Lot the nephew of Abraham was captured. A lot of people reading this are going through pain because of wrong choices they have made. It is said that we are a product of the choices we make, where we are, is determined to a great extent by the choices we make. Your dreams may look shattered because of some mistakes you made in your life, nevertheless you should not allow your past to define you, you can move beyond the mistakes of yesterday. When the hand of the Lord comes upon you, your past mistakes are overruled by the mercies of the Lord.

Lot found himself in the valley of Siddim because of the choice he made when Abraham presented him with a decision to choose where he wanted to go. Lot's decision was motivated by what he saw with his natural eyes. Many people have made wrong choices because of a mirage, something that looked promising but it was a scum.

Robert Liardon in his book "God's Generals" shares the account of Kathryn Kuhlman making a mistake by marrying a man that had left his wife and children, he records that "the work Kathryn had so diligently built over the previous five years quickly disintegrated. Hewitt bought out Kathryn's share of the building, and Helen went to work for a smaller church in Denver. The "sheep" scattered. Because of this grievous mistake, Kathryn lost her church, her close friends, and her ministry. Even her relationship with God suffered because Kathryn put "Mister" and his desires over her passion for God." (Liardon, 1996, 256). Kathryn Kuhlman went through pain because of wrong choices she made but when she appealed to the mercies of God, He had mercy on her and released His hand on her life. This resulted in her dream being restored. When the hand of God locates your life, even the valley of Siddim will be turned into a blessed place.

There are some key decisions that we need to be careful to ponder on when making because if we make a wrong move, we will end up in the valley of Siddim. I will share some of these key decisions, and if you are caught in the valley of Siddim, you will see what you need to do to come out of this place of pain.

Core Values

According to the Business Dictionary, values are "important and lasting beliefs or ideals shared by the members of a culture about what is good or bad and desirable or undesirable." Values have great influence on a person's behaviour and attitudes, they guide our daily lives; they explain why we do what we do. Our values will determine whether we find ourselves in the valley of Siddim or not. The values we have affect the choices we make; our values will determine who we marry, who our close friends are, and many other areas of our lives. This is why it is important to choose values that bring advancement in our lives

Some of the key values that we need to avoid being trapped in the valley of Siddim are: integrity; being passionate about our assignment in life; hard work; accountability; and value for relationships

Your Life Partner

Many people are in pain today because of the people they chose to marry. Esau lost the favour he had with his father Isaac because of the women he married. Solomon had his kingship destroyed because of the women he married. I know people that moved under the power of God before marrying but today the story is different. One of my friends was told by someone close to him that he would have gone far if it was not for the woman he married.

If you find yourself in the valley of Siddim because of mistakes in the area of marriage, you can cry out to God, He will help you; He cares for you. (Psalm 55:22)

Your Close Friends

Someone has said that "show me your friends and I will predict your future." Who you decide to have as your close friend will determine where you end up in life. Many people are stuck in the valley of Siddim and when they look at their lives, it is easy for them to conclude that things got destroyed after an encountered with someone who had no fear for God.

The Bible says that a companion of fools shall be destroyed (Proverbs 13:20). If you choose to walk with the wicked, you will end up in the valley of Siddim. He who walks with prostitutes will lose his/her wealth (Proverbs 29:3). No matter how powerful you are, wrong choices will cause you to lose everything you have worked for. Lot went to Sodom with a lot of wealth but lost everything he had labored for because of wrong choices.

Your Career

God has created each one of us with a specific purpose. Each one of us has a gift that can cause us to excel in life if developed. No one is a mistake, you are not a mistake; you are special in the eyes of God.

While it is true that we are special and carry a seed of greatness, we are not called to do the same things. The eyes and the nose are very different but both are important to the body. Do not choose a career because of what people say, you need to examine your strengths and do what you are equipped to do.

Your Daily Routine

What you choose to do on a daily basis will determine whether you remain in the valley of Siddim or not. Archbishop Duncan Williams says that life does not give us what we deserve but what we fight for. This means that if we do not make a decision to fight for our lives, we will remain in pain, in the valley of Siddim, while carrying great promises.

Some of the things that we need to do on a daily basis to keep ourselves from the valley of Siddim are:

> ➤ *Studying of the Word of God*

The word of God is life (see John 6:63), as we feed on the word, we are built and equipped to succeed in life (Joshua 1: 7-8; Psalm 1: 1-3). Spend time studying the word of God on a daily basis and you will be empowered to avoid the valley of Siddim, or empowered to get out.

> ➤ *Servicing Our Altar*

The strength of our prayer altars determines our authority level in the spiritual world. God has called us to a life of power but if we become strangers to the prayer altar, we will be bound by satanic forces. The altar is a place of spiritual power, a place where the spiritual world is permitted to intervene in the physical. The strength of your altar will determine whether you remain in the valley of Siddim or not. The fire on the altar must always be kept burning (Leviticus 6:12-13), in the New Testament, the Bible says that we must always service the prayer altar, we must pray without ceasing. (1 Thessalonians 5:17)

H.E. Schmul in his book "Handbook on Revival" records that *"David Brainerd decided to give himself unreservedly to intercessory prayer. It is said that 'whole nights were spent in agonizing prayer in the dark woods, his clothes drenched with the sweat of his travail.' Suddenly the Spirit was poured upon the whole region of Susquehanna. His first audience there had consisted of four women and a few children. Now there came streaming upon him from all sides a host of men and women, who pressed upon him, and grasping the bridle of his horse, besought him with intense earnestness to tell them the way of salvation."*

I remember a time I found myself in the valley of Siddim because of some wrong decisions I had made. I felt like it was over with me, things were tough and seemed hopeless. I had resigned from ministry and my body was battling with sicknesses. In the midst of my pain, I decided to do something that had helped me in my earlier years in my Christian walk, I serviced my prayer altar with prayer and fasting, and before long God opened doors for me to serve Him, He blessed me so much, no man could have done what He has done for me. Prayer got me out of the valley of Siddim.

We can never get out of the valley of Siddim if we are strangers to prayer and fasting; daily fellowship with the Holy Spirit on the prayer altar will benefit us more than anything we can ever think of. Motivation speaking is great but it can never deliver us from satanic forces that are determined to keep us in the valley of Siddim. Let us go to the prayer altar on a daily basis and no power of hell will be able to stop us.

One man that greatly blessed the body of Christ in the early years of the 20th century was a man called Smith Wigglesworth. The man lacked formal education but he spent time on the prayer altar and wherever he went, demonic forces were subdued. In his book, "Greater Worker: Experiencing God's Power," Smith Wigglesworth describing an encounter he had before praying for a man who was dying said *"At eight o'clock they said to me, "Have a little refreshment." But I have found prayer and fasting the greatest joy, and you will always find it so when you are led by God." (Wigglesworth, 20).*

Prayer and fasting was the joy of Smith Wigglesworth and mighty miracles followed his life. Spend time praying and fasting on a regular basis and you will never be stuck in any valley of Siddim.

> ### *Reading Great Books*

Someone once said that readers are leaders. The Bible helps us understand that Paul excelled in his assignment because he gave attention to reading of books (2 Timothy 4: 13). If you desire to be relevant to your generation, give time to fellowship with the Holy Spirit and reading of books.

When you read books, you will discover information that will cause you to get out of the valley of Siddim. The Bible tells us that the truth we know shall set us free (John :32), it will keep us from the valley of pain, whatever you are going through today, find books that will give you information that brings you freedom.

I once heard someone saying that "if you want to hide something from an African, put it in writing." Many people are in the valley of pain because of bad reading habits. Decide to improve yourself by reading wide and writing down the lessons learnt. One of the best prayers you can use on a weekly basis is "Lord show me and lead me to a book that will change my life for the better."

Your daily routine can help you avoid the valley of Siddim and if you are already in this valley, what you do on a daily basis will cause you to either get out or remain there. Create time on a daily basis to study the Bible, fellowshipping with the Holy Spirit, and reading of books that help you improve in your area of operation.

Your Relationship with Jesus

John 14: 6 shows us that Jesus is the way, the truth, and the life. The valley of Siddim is presented as a difficult place but there is a place that is worse than this place, it is called hell. Hell is real and it is a terrible place that you must avoid at all cost. Today, preachers don't want to talk about hell claiming that it threatens people, causing them to respond to the gospel out of fear. It is important that people are told the whole truth. If you have not accepted Jesus as your personal Lord and Saviour, you will end up in a place of pain. There is life after death, it does not matter what you believe, the word of God is real and a valley more painful than the valley of Siddim is a place where all who rejects Jesus will end up.

Paul in the book of Romans shows us that all have sinned (Romans 3: 23), and in the book of John, we have seen that Jesus is the way to the Father. John further tells us that all that received Him (Jesus) were given power to be called the children of God (John 1:12). You can avoid hell, the place of eternal condemnation, by accepting Jesus Christ as your personal Lord and Saviour.

CHAPTER TWO

THE VALLEY OF ELAH

1 Sam 17:17-19
*Then Jesse said to his son David, "Take now for your brothers…. Now Saul and they and all the men of Israel were in the **Valley of Elah**, fighting with the Philistines. NKJV*

There was a season in my life when I was experiencing so much pain, I didn't want to go to Church but being a pastor of the Church, I was forced to attend Church services and preach. On one of those days, I preached a sermon in which I cried out my heart to God. The title of the sermon was "DOES IT PAY TO BE GOOD?"

The second valley is called the valley of Elah. It is the valley where the enemy desires to kill you before your full potential manifests. This is the valley where David killed the giant Goliath that had threatened the children of Israel. In the valley of Siddim, people experience pain because of wrong choices, in the valley of Elah; people experience pain because the enemy wants to stop them from progressing.

Many people are asking themselves questions as to why they have to go through battle after battle; many are wondering what wrong they have done to continuously go through pain.

In 1999 and 2000, things were extremely tough for me; I thought that I was the greatest fool that ever lived; everything I tried to do ended up in pain. I prayed, fasted, and even repented for sins I did not commit but still the situations remained the same. I didn't know then that I was going through the valley of Elah.

The Bible tells us that David arrived in the valley of Elah at a time when the children of Israel were in deep trouble, an enemy, stronger than them, was challenging them and they did not know what to do. Saul tried to encourage his troops by promising some good incentives to anyone who would destroy the nation's rival

(Goliath) but to no avail, no one was willing to risk his life.

You might be in such a situation and you don't know what to do, you have walked in integrity but things keep getting worse, you are in the valley of Elah. God will see you through, just keep trusting Him (Galatians 6:9). There was a season in my life when I was experiencing so much pain, I didn't want to go to Church but being a pastor of the Church, I was forced to attend Church services and preach. On one of those days, I preached a sermon in which I cried out my heart to God. The title of the sermon was "**DOES IT PAY TO BE GOOD?**" Whatever situation that you are going through today, Call on the name of the Lord (see Jeremiah 33:3).

Before I show you more information about the battles of the valley of Elah, may I remind you that God is faithful; He is dependable. You have encountered this book because God wants you to know that He cares for you, He desires to help you, if you can only trust Him, strength will come upon you and you will overcome every power that stands against your progress.

The valley of Elah is a place of discouragement. When David thought of challenging Goliath, well experienced people in that field told him that he did not have what it took to fight the giant that was threatening the people of God. Many gifted people are stuck in the valley of Elah because they do not want to appear unrealistic. A lot of people have abandoned their dreams because of the discouragement they got from well-meaning people as well as experts in that field. But I am encouraging you that you have what it takes to do more than you have done, just call on the name of the Lord and He will give you strength

The Bible tells us that it is impossible to please God without faith (Hebrews11:6). Discouragement has an assignment to destroy our faith in God. To fight discouragement, spend time studying the word of God that is able to build you (Acts 20:32); have regular times of prayer and fasting (Matthew 17: 20-21); spend most of your prayer time praying in tongues (Jude 20). If you do these three things on a regular basis, faith shall be built in your heart and the enemy shall be destroyed.

The valley of Elah is a place of intimidation. When David thought of fighting Goliath, he was told that he was too small to fight the Philistine champion. Many people reading this book have been intimidated into giving up on the dream that was so dear to them. The experts told you that it could not be done and you gave up on your God given dream.

In the valley of Elah, many voices will be screaming at you telling you that you do not have what it takes to accomplish what you desire to do. You are just a youth, what can you do? You will hear voices tell you to sit down because you are a woman, or because you are a divorcee. You might be reading this and you have been told that your sickness has no cure and many of your close friends are telling you to accept your situation.

Your situation is not beyond the reach of the Holy Spirit, He is able to transform your life. In June 2018, I was preaching in a certain village within Luapula province of Zambia, I was told about a lady that had eye complications. In the morning session as I was praying for the sick, I told this lady that during the afternoon session, she was going to come back with a testimony. Before preaching the word in the afternoon session, I asked the lady to give us a testimony and she shared with us how God had set her completely free. The experts might have told you that they is no cure for your situation, fear not, our miracle working God is setting you free right now. The word of God is coming alive in your spirit and every sickness is being destroyed in the mighty name of Jesus. The entrance of God's word brings light, when light comes, darkness has to leave (Psalm 19:130). Every work of darkness in your life shall be destroyed by the power of light, the power of the word of God.

In the valley of Elah, you need to know the power of sacrifice to overcome satanic forces. The language of the supernatural is a language of sacrifice. Every throne is sustained by an altar; the power of your altar is determined by the value of the sacrifice offered on it. If your altar is weak, you cannot silence the voice of your Goliath. Many people do not know how to handle occultic forces because of a lack of understanding of the power that is in sacrificial living. Your sacrifice attracts the hand of God to intervene in your situation

Goliath was a seasoned warrior who was also an idol worshiper, when he faced David, the Bible says that he cursed David by his gods (1 Samuel

17:43); though Goliath was a powerful warrior, he knew that battles must first be won in the spiritual before the physical. The people that you are fighting with in the market place and many other places have raised altars and offered costly sacrifices just to silence you. In the book of Numbers we see how Balak hired a prophet to curse the children of Israel before engaging them in battle, he promised to richly reward the prophet, and when altars were raised on the mountain, seven bulls and seven rams had to be carried to the mountain where they were to be sacrificed (Numbers 22-23). There are forces that are strategising on how to destroy you without your knowledge but if your prayer altar is active; God will silence your enemies without your knowledge in some cases.

Because David knew the power of sacrifice, he approached Goliath in a sacrificial manner; nothing mattered to him but the honour of the name of the Lord. He sacrificed his relationship with Eliab his elder brother. With due respect, he refused to allow his brother to stop him from doing what he believed was the best for Israel. David also offered his life as a living sacrifice consecrated to God. He chose to honour the name of the Lord above everything else. David was dead to self; nothing in this life mattered to him more than bringing glory to the name of the Lord.

May every giant in your life be destroyed as you choose to honour the name of the Lord in every situation, sickness shall leave your body; past failures shall be overturned in the name of Jesus. Any area of your life that has come under a satanic spell, causing you to accept defeat without a fight is being set free right now. Come out of the valley of Elah today! Victory is your portion, the giant of sicknesses, financial giants and all kinds of giants are falling down.

One great thing about the battles of the valley of Elah is that you receive life transforming rewards. The rewards you get after the victory in this valley are rewards that keep coming to you for the rest of your life. In my season of pain, I struggled with sicknesses and when I got the victory, I was ushered into a healing ministry that has seen many people being healed in a lot of places

I grew up with the pain of not knowing my father and when God called me into ministry, satanic voices spoke to me telling me that I did not qualify to serve God because of my past. The devil brought thoughts that tried to stop what God has called me into by discouraging me. He said that I was unworthy due to my past failures and experiences. But God brought healing in my heart and sent me to take the message of emotional healing to my generation. God gave me victory over my emotional brokenness and the reward has been that many people keep receiving healing as I minister in a number of places.

You will not be destroyed, don't give up, I speak God's supernatural favour that causes us to possess our possessions to come upon you now in a mighty way. Choose to trust God in every situation (Psalm 44:1-8)

CHAPTER THREE

THE VALLEY OF BACA

As they pass through the Valley of Baca,
They make it a spring;
The rain also covers it with pools.Psalm 84:6 NKJV

Emotional pain is real, that is why when you are hurting don't pretend as though all is well; pain will kill you if you don't call on the name of the Lord. James says "is anyone in pain? Let him pray" (James 5:13). Complaining is not the biblical solution to your pain, prayer is the only way out of deep pain.

The third valley is the valley of Baca; it is the valley of weeping. The word Baca means weeping. The valley of Baca is a place of tears, suffering, and sorrows. Baca is a place of deep pain due to betrayal, rejection, and disappointment. It is believed that when David was running away from Absalom his son, he passed through this valley. It is a place of deep emotional pain. It is also said that the valley of Baca was prone to long periods of droughts.

There was a time in my ministry when I came across a family that had a suicide case every year. About six key family members had committed suicide in six years. This was a satanic design that covered the family to be in the valley of Baca, and to be in tears always. Another family had a curse that never allowed anyone to spend more than three years in marriage. Every member of the family experienced divorce after three years of marriage.

Almost everyone has experienced the pain of the valley of Baca, the important thing as the Psalmist said while going through the valley, is to pass through and not to remain in it. In the book of Job, we read that Job feared God and shunned evil; however, this man that walked in holiness found himself experiencing the pain of Baca. Emotional pain is real, that is why when you are hurting don't pretend as though all is well; pain will kill you if you don't call on the name of the Lord. James says "is anyone in pain? Let him pray" (James 5:13). Complaining is not the biblical solution to your pain, prayer is the only way out of deep pain.

Many things cause us to find ourselves in the valley of Baca, these include the following:

Betrayal

The Vocabulary Dictionary defines betrayal as "an act of deliberate disloyalty. Betrayal's root is betray, which comes from the middle English word bitrayen- meaning 'mislead, deceive,' betrayal has to do with destroying someone's trust, possibly by lying." David experienced the pain of betrayal in the valley of Baca, when his own biological son decided to take over the kingdom by force.

We experience betrayal in many areas of our lives. Someone promised to marry you and you loved him/her so much but only to discover that he/she is having an affair with your best friend. You shared some personal information with a friend or a pastor but surprisingly you hear people talking about what you had shared in confidence openly and you are hurting because you feel what you shared was personal information. It may also be that someone presented what looked like a great business idea but today you have lost everything, because you did not know that it was just a scum. So many situations have caused people to feel betrayed. So many people are hurting without anyone knowing because of failing to deal with the pain of the valley of Baca, the pain of betrayal. Your friend, your pastor, your spouse, and many other people you trusted hurt you and you are still hanging in the pain of yesterday as you have refused to forgive. One thing that I should share with you is that failure to deal with the pain of the valley of Baca will cause you to remain stuck in this terrible place. Mark shows us that failure to let go of the pain of yesterday will hinder the miracle of today.

Mark 11: 25 "And whenever you stand praying, if you have anything against anyone, forgive him that your Father in heaven may also forgive you your trespasses. 26.But if you do not forgive, neither will your Father in heaven forgive your trespasses."

Rejection

Rejection is defined as the act of refusing to accept or believe someone or something. The best example that comes to my mind is the story of Jephthah in the book of Judges (Judges 11). Jephthah was rejected by his family; they called him all kinds of names. Even though you may have been rejected by people you loved and respected, like Jephthah, know that God is able to transform your situation. David faced the rejection of his son as he passed through the valley of Baca, he faced insults from people that had a grudge against him (2 Samuel16: 5-11).

I have gone through the pain of rejection and I know the deadly effect it has on both our physical life and our emotions. There was a time when I faced sicknesses that could not respond to medication, but the moment I chose to forgive the people that had hurt me, the sicknesses were all healed. Rejection is painful and you may feel like you are justified to be bitter towards those that offended you. Take your issue to the Lord in prayer; God is able to bring healing in your heart.

I have a friend who also came across a bitter situation in his life. This friend had related with a certain lady for close to ten years; plans of their wedding were advancing pretty well. A few days after burying his closest brother, the lady informed him that she had changed her mind about getting married to him because she was concerned about his character. Upon trying to find out what she meant and what the matter really was, the lady said that she could not get married to a man whom she had never seen angry, she said that people who don't show emotions of anger are dangerous people. My friend was seriously hurt and instead of dealing with the pain, he decided to cover it and pretended as though he was not affected.

After some time, this friend of mine met another lady and they loved each other. But guess what? The problem that the second lady faced with this friend of mine was the anger he exhibited towards her. One time she told him that she had never seen a person who is easily angered like him. The issue here was that this friend of mine was still battling with the rejection of the first relationship. This clearly shows that rejection if not dealt with will cause us to remain stuck in the valley of Baca.

Disappointment

Disappointment is the feeling of displeasure caused by the non-fulfillment of our hopes or expectations. Some disappointments may not cause us to be stuck in the valley of Baca but some are deadly. Disappointments cause us to ask many questions that bring pain and bitterness. In 2001, I was pastor of a Church in Lusaka and in this Church; I met people that never trusted pastors because of what they had witnessed. One lady kept asking me "how can pastors fight on the altar." She was referring to a situation that happened in the Church she attended before joining us. The disappointment that this lady experienced caused her a lot of pain that needed the touch of the hand of God to heal.

Some have experienced disappointment in the area of marriage, things have not happened as expected, other are disappointed because of failure in the business world while others face disappointment in many other areas. The way out of this kind of pain is to call on the name of Jesus.

Some people are secretly frustrated because of unfulfilled secret expectations. You are disappointed that the person you secretly admired married someone else, let go of the pain, God will see you through; your miracle is waiting for you to let go of your past.

Joseph Scriven experienced a lot of painful things that could have left him bitter and disappointed with God. It is said that on the eve of his wedding, his fiancée drowned and died. He left Ireland and settled in Canada so that he could be far from the place of pain. While in Canada, he engaged another lady, but his fiancée fell sick and died before they could be married.

Scriven received news that his mother was sick in Ireland. He could not afford the cost to return to Ireland, so he decided to send a poem to his mother to comfort her. In his poem, he did not complain about God or what he had gone through, instead he chose to put his trust in God. He declared in his poem that "what a friend we have in Jesus, oh what pains and grief we bear, oh because we do not carry, everything to God in prayer...." The poem has become one of the most treasured songs in the Christian world because someone who experienced disappointment after disappointment refused to be bitter. Take your issue to God and He will carry you through the valley of Baca.

When you put your trust in God while experiencing pain, you will attract the hand of God on your life. The hand of the Lord is able to transform the valley of Baca into a spring of Joy. Let go of the pain of your past and receive the healing power of God's love. Today, the hand of God shall turn your valley of Baca into a spring of joy. Psalm 84: 5 – 6 tells us that those who trust in God shall make the valley of Baca a spring. Don't give up; you will receive strength to turn Baca into a miracle. Your situation is about to change for the better.

CHAPTER FOUR

THE VALLEY OF ACHOR

I will give her her vineyards from there,
*And the **Valley of Achor** as a*
door of hope. Hosea 2:14-15 *NKJV*

God in Hosea 2:15 promises to make the valley of Achor into a door of hope. Whatever has been a source of pain in your life shall be turned into a source of blessing. Your trouble shall be turned to joy in the mighty name of Jesus!

The fourth valley is the valley of Achor. The word Achor in Hebrew means trouble. The valley of Achor is a valley of life threatening troubles. It is a place of extreme problems. It is a valley of always labouring but nothing to show for the labour, a place where people are always crying and feel empty. The valley of Achor is a place where life seems to be hopeless and bitter. It is the valley of the shadow of death.

People find themselves in this valley as a result of disobeying God. It is in this valley that Achan was killed because he troubled the nation of Israel (Joshua 7:24-26). I experienced this kind of pain when I was in Bible School in 2001, God gave me an instruction and I chose to do what I thought was a better decision; I suffered for almost a year and almost lost my life. God had mercy on me and gave me another instruction that brought instant healing when I obeyed

Why are you where you are today? If you know that the reason for your pain is disobedience in your life, I call you to repentance before it is too late. I have prayed that God will place this book in the hands of someone who needs to make things right with God, God loves you so much, and He desires to bring restoration in your life as you respond to Him in repentance. Let us look at Hosea chapter two and see some of the occurrences that people in the valley of Achor experience. Prayerfully read through these occurrences and make the right decision if you discover that these things are describing your situation

Loss of Direction. Hosea 2:6

Many people find themselves in situations where they do not know where they are going or how to come out of challenging situations. God tells the children of Israel that He was "... going to fence her in with thorn bushes and build a wall to block her way" (Good News Bible). If you do not repent in the valley of Achor, you will die with depression because of the many challenges that will be coming one after another with no solution in sight.

Often times we hear people saying that they do not know what to do when faced with a challenge. In many of such cases, no solution can be found because these situations are permitted by God due to disobedience. Disobedience always empowers satanic forces to block our ways.

Are you in a situation where you are stuck and you don't know what to do? Is there something in your life that you know of that has caused your way to be blocked. Repent and allow the blood of Jesus to cleanse you from all manner of unrighteousness (Hebrews 9:14)

Loss of Provision. Hosea 2:9

So many people do not realise that God is the one who has caused them to possess what they have. In Hosea 2:8 God says that Israel did not acknowledge that her provision came from God, because of this, she went into idolatry. As a result of this, God promised to withdraw His provision from this people.

Many people are experiencing financial challenges because they are in the valley of Achor where provision is withheld. Everything they try to do crumbles down because in this valley God allows the enemy to afflict His children (Haggai 1:1-15).

So many people have allowed pride to enter their hearts, they feel that the possessions they have are a result of their own doing. There are pastors who seem to be prospering while living in sin and they think that nothing can stop them. Child of God sin will usher you into the valley of Achor, you will lose everything you have in a moment; you will not know what has hit your wealth. Sin is terrible, I have seen people reduced to nothing with no one to help them, remember if you choose to continue walking in sin, your sin will speak against you (Numbers 32:23).

Loss of Protection. Hosea 2:10

Ecclesiastes 10:8says that anyone who breaks through a wall

shall be bitten by a snake. A wall speaks of protection while a snake speaks of satanic powers. Anyone who breaks a wall will be destroyed by the devil. When you resist the warnings of God and find yourself in the valley of Achor, no one can deliver you, you have no protection. The valley of Achor is a terrible place where people are defenseless; they are at the mercy of satanic forces.

In the book of Judges, we read about a man by the name of Samson, he played with sin for a long time until the wall of protection around his life was broken, his life ended in a miserable way. If you see that the walls of protection around your life are destroyed, cry out to God for mercy and He will answer you

Loss of Peace and Joy. Hosea 2:11

There is no peace in the valley of Achor, no joyful celebrations. The valley of Achor is a place of pain and depression. You are reading this and you know that people admire you but deep in your heart you know that you have no peace, come to the altar and lay your burden on Jesus. Jesus loves you, he cares about your destiny, come out of that life of pretence and let Jesus give you the peace that surpasses human understanding

Proverbs 14:13 says that "even in laughter, the heart may sorrow and the end of mirth *(celebrations)* may be grief" (NKJV). Many people are crying in their heart but appear to be enjoying life, it seems as though all is well but when no one is watching, they are asking themselves "how will I ever come out of this mess." Be real, take off your mask, Jesus wants to help you out of your painful situation, call on Him today.

Loss of Businesses. Hosea 2:12

God says that He will destroy the things that the children of Israel trusted in, he was going to destroy their businesses. Businesses do not survive in the valley of Achor regardless of the connections you have. Many people have lost businesses because of disobeying the voice of God. I believe a number of us know of people who had successful business that got destroyed because the owner lost the fear for God. What you build using the altar of God can only be sustained by the altar of God, never abandon God when He blesses you.

Dear child of God, regardless of where you are today, regardless of what you have done in life, God is calling you to Himself. In Hosea 2:14, God promises to draw His children to a place where He can restore them. He says that He will bring them to the wilderness and speak comfort to them. In the place of pain, God gives His children a word with the power to bring them out of the valley of Achor.

The way out of the valley of Achor is through the word of God, you need to receive a word from God that shall destroy every satanic cage over your life.

When you embrace the word of God in your situation, your valley of Achor shall be turned into a door of hope. God in Hosea 2:15 promises to make the valley of Achor into a door of hope. Whatever has been a source of pain in your life shall be turned into a source of blessing. Your trouble shall be turned to joy in the mighty name of Jesus! I speak open doors for everyone reading this word with faith in the faithfulness of our God; your miracle shall manifest in the mighty name of Jesus.

CHAPTER FIVE

THE VALLEY DRY BONES

*The hand of the Lord came upon me and brought me out in the Spirit of the Lord, **and set me down in the midst of the valley;** and it was full of bones. Ezekiel 37:1 NKJV*

I like saying that you are not destroyed because of witches or challenges; it is a lack of knowledge that destroys people. Isaiah 5: 13 says that my people have gone into captivity because they have no knowledge.

The fifth valley is the valley of dry bones. This valley presents a picture of hopelessness. It is in this valley where dreams and visions are buried. It is a valley where men and women of great potential remain stuck and are in a state of despair. The challenges of this valley seem to be insurmountable, challenges that cause many to conclude that they can never be overcome.

Many people are hurting because of a sense of hopelessness. I know pastors that preach powerfully but whose churches have so many problems that the pastor feels hopeless. Many pastors are in the valley of hopelessness, the dream they had to reach the world with the

Gospel of Jesus Christ has been shattered by different painful experiences. To any pastor going through the valley of dry bones, don't give up; call on the name of the Lord. He will restore you and empower you to experience victories in the area of your calling.

Like the valley of Achor, people find themselves in the valley of dry bones because of disobedience. The difference is that in the valley of dry bones, the cause of the pain is the sin of our fathers. The Bible shows us the pain experienced by the children of Israel during the time of Jeremiah was due to the sins of their fathers (Lamentations 5:7). The sins of our fathers cause satan to establish a satanic pattern in the lives of the people that can never be changed without divine intervention. Many people are in pain today and do not even know why things don't seem to work for them, they are in the valley of dry bones   .

Many people are convinced that their situation cannot be changed, like the children of Israel (Ezekiel 37:11), they are convinced that they cannot be delivered from the powers that hold them captive. God is a mighty God, nothing is impossible with Him, if you can call on Him today, He will transform your situation. Bishop Oyedepo says that God is the "Unchangeable Changer." He does not change (Malachi 3:6); He is still the miracle working God. Your situation is not beyond His reach, open your heart to receive His word and your life will never be the same. I like saying that you are not destroyed because of witches or challenges; it is a lack of knowledge that destroys people. Many people have gone into captivity because they have no knowledge (Isaiah 5: 13). May you receive the word that carries your miracle today.

You might be in the valley of dry bones right now, your story will change. We experience the valley of dry bones in many areas of our lives; I will outline a few that I have encountered as I have been serving God in ministry.

In the Area of Education

In 2015, I prayed for a young lady who was studying at one of the secondary schools in Samfya. She was under a satanic family spell that did not allow any family member to complete grade eleven. Every time she went to school, she fell seriously sick and would work up in a hospital bed. When I interviewed her, I discovered that her elder brother had similar experiences when he was in grade eleven and had to drop out of school for him to remain health. I prayed for her, breaking the powers of the enemy that had established a pattern of educational failure in the family. In 2016, she wrote her grade twelve exams, the first one in the family to do that.

I prayed for a young man in Ndola who used to get sick every time it was exam period. He missed three exams in three years because of a satanic spell, when that power was broken, he came out of the valley of dry bones; he wrote his exams and managed to clear all the courses he sat for.

If you have been operating under a spell that tempers with your education, I speak freedom today; every satanic curse of educational failure in your life is broken in the name of Jesus. I call you to apply yourself to the discipline required for educational success; every power that kept your family members in educational bondage is broken in the name of Jesus.

In the Area of Marriage

A friend of mine had been in more than ten relationships, all of which ended unexpectedly, he could not explain why this was happening to him. He came to me one time and said "I think I am not meant to marry." He reached this conclusion because of repeated failures. When we looked at his family, it was discovered that all the males in the family either don't marry or marry when they are almost forty years old.

I met a family in Samfya that operated under a curse in the area of marriage, every member of the family that got married experienced divorce after three years of marriage. These are cases that need the hand of God to be revealed before you give marital counseling. I heard of a man that had raised an evil altar where he would go and declare that "I scatter any man getting close to my daughters." The daughters had good jobs, well-mannered but could not get married. When the curse was broken, two daughters got married in the same year, and the father's businesses had problems after problems. When the father got saved, he confessed that he had a covenant that his business would only remain successful if his daughters remained single.

A young lady came to see me complaining that any man that showed interest in marrying her would break the engagement a week before the wedding. Three men had done that to her, each one said that she was a good person but they could not marry her because they had lost interest.

In the mighty name of Jesus, I break every marital spell working against your life and family, every evil covenant made that fights your marital destiny is broken by the blood of Jesus. Every satanic voice speaking against your marriage is silenced by the voice of the blood of Jesus.

In Business

I know someone whose father had a successful business; he was admired by many people in town because of the wealth he had and also how his family life was. At a time we all thought the man was reaching his peak, things began to go wrong, issues of huge debts surfaced and before long the business was destroyed. The man left town and needed his children to take care of him. One of his sons also had a successful business but went through the same thing the man went through, the son has lost his business and is depending on well-wishes.

Many people have great business ideas and the discipline to

have a successful business but because of unbroken curses operating in the family, they fail to establish anything. The children of Israel were in pain because the hand of the Lord was against them. If the hand of the Lord is working against you, your business can never have a breakthrough, it will experience loses. Some people are operating under a satanic spell because of the sins of their parents, evil covenants that your fathers established might be working against your business, break the covenants and you will operate under an open heaven.

In the Area of Employment

A young man graduated as one of the best graduates at a university in

Nairobi, Kenya but could not get a job for over fifteen years. He was the first person in his family to graduate from a university but the enemy could not allow him to get employed. He received prayer, the satanic cage that kept the family in bondage was broken and within a week he managed to get a job.

I heard of a man that was stuck in the valley of dry bones in the area of employment, he had very good papers from the University of Zambia but struggled to get a job. His father was a witchdoctor and none of the children got employed, they could get all manner of qualifications from the best universities but could not get employed. This man was led to the

Lord Jesus Christ and all satanic covenants that held the family in bondage were destroyed. Today the man has a good job working as a senior officer in one of the ministries in the government of Zambia.

Are you working hard and others get recognised for your labours? Are you always overlooked in the area of employment even when you are the best at your work? Are you struggling to get a job even though you have great qualifications? What is your situation in the area of employment? Today, you can be set free from every satanic spell that has left your family in the valley of dry bones. The way out of this valley is through the word of God, the word is light and when light comes, darkness must leave without any struggle. May the word of God come alive in your spirit today, may you come out of the valley of dry bones in the mighty name of Jesus.

In the Area of Health

In the book of 2 Kings 5: 27, we read about the case of Gehazi who was cursed by Elisha because of the sin of covetousness in his life. Elisha said that the leprosy of Naaman was going to cling to Gehazi and his family forever. Can you imagine the grand children of Gehazi trying to figure out why they always had a case of leprosy in their family. Because of the sin of Gehazi, his family had a health issue that didn't respond to medication.

I heard a pastor speaking in a conference saying that in his family, anybody that got to the age of thirty would get sick and die. When he gave his life to Jesus, he spent time on the prayer altar breaking all satanic covenants that operated in the family and God set his family free, today the pastor is over forty years because he encountered the power of the Lord that is able to change any valley of dry bones into a place of great joy

Any sickness that holds your family in bondage is been destroyed right now in the mighty name of Jesus, whatever you have considered irreversible in your life shall be reversed in the mighty name of Jesus. As you read this, I command every sickness in your body to disappear in the name of Jesus. Every satanic decree of premature death in your family shall be broken as you submit yourself to the power of the word of God. Every form of misfortune projected into your life due to the mistakes of your forefathers shall be erased by the power of the blood of Jesus.

No matter how dark your dream seems to be, don't give up, just call on the name of the Lord and He will see you through. God wants you to call on Him so He can release His hand of miracles on all you do. In your education, God wants to show you His greatness; in business, politics, and marriage etc., the hand of the Lord at work in your life is all you need to experience victory. Don't look to man; put your trust in God (See Jeremiah 17:5-8). Today as you respond to the word of God in your situation, God will step into your situation and something beautiful will come out of your life regardless of where you are today. God will favour you causing you to possess all that He has promised (see Psalm 44:1-8).

CONCLUSION

When the children of Israel were threatened with destruction in the book of Esther, they fasted before God to overturn the satanic decree (see Esther 4:16-17). Every valley you have found yourself in shall be turned into a door of hope as you choose to address your issue on the altar of prayer and fasting.

What kind of valley have you gone through or are you in? Why are you doing what you are doing? Are you happy with your life? Are you where you think you should be in life? Can your situation change? Can your dream live again? God is able to change your situation, He is the Omni-potent one, nothing takes Him by surprise and nothing is difficult for Him.

It does not matter what kind of valley you are in, God loves you so much and He is calling you out of that place of pain. The word you have encountered in this book is the word God has sent to help you out of that valley of pain. You cannot be destroyed by any satanic power if you choose to remain under the protection of our living God. There are three things that you need to have dominion over the devil; three things that have helped me turn the valleys of my life into a door of hope.

Consecration

Consecration has to do with denying your body the opportunity to gratify its lusts. It is choosing to please God instead of indulging in personal pleasures. The Bible says that sin shall no longer have dominion over you (Romans 6:14), consecration has to do with forsaking all sin and weights (Hebrews 12:1) that slows us down in our pursuit of God. Consecration causes the power of God to be made manifest in our lives

Prayer and Fasting

Fasting has to do with denying your body food. Fasting coupled with prayer causes demonic bondages to be broken. Satanic decrees made against your life can easily be broken on the altar of prayer and fasting. When the children of Israel were threatened with destruction in the book of Esther, they fasted before God to overturn the satanic decree (see Esther 4:16-17). Every valley you have found yourself in shall be turned into a door of hope as you choose to address your issue on the altar of prayer and fasting.

A Life of Sacrifices

Sacrifice has to do with denying yourself what you would do with your money or other treasured goods. The value of your sacrifice on the altar determines the power of your altar. If you are a stranger to sacrifice, you will be a stranger to dominion in the spiritual realms. In 2 Samuel 24:17-18, David cried out to God because of the plague that was destroying the land and God responded by asking him to build an altar and offer a sacrifice. Your life of sacrifice will cause you to turn any valley into a place of joy.

May you receive grace to live a life that is consecrated to God; a life that regularly spends time on the altar having prayer and fasting; and may you live your life in a sacrificial manner.

Other Books by
MkambanizitheDaka

- Destined For Greatness
- When Your Dream Becomes A Nightmare
- Your Dream Shall Live Again

Made in the USA
Columbia, SC
05 March 2023

13265570R00057